# F is for Food Forest

## An ABC Book from Wisconsin Food Forests

# Un bosque de alimentos

## Un libro ABC de Wisconsin Food Forests

Written by: Emily Steinwehe and
Erin McWalter
Illustrated by: Emily Marie Schroeder

## Dedicated to

the 11 federally recognized & 3 unrecognized
First Nation Tribes of Wisconsin
who were our first teachers
of sustainability and who continue to take care of
our beautiful native plants today.

&

Rodney Volkmar and Madelon Wise
for their immeasurable help during our first years of
Wisconsin Food Forests

# Words to Know

**Annual** (of a plant) living for a year or less, perpetuating itself by seed.

Anual (de una planta) periodo de un año de vida o menos, se puede perpetuar a sí misma a través de la semilla.

**Groundcover** low-growing, spreading plants that help to stop weeds from growing.

Cobertura del suelo: plantas que no crecen muy alto y se expanden para detener el crecimiento de malas hierbas.

**Native** (of a plant or animal) of indigenous origin or growth.

Nativo (de una planta o animal) de origen o crecimiento indígena.

**Perennial** (of a plant) living for several years.

Perenne (de una planta) que vive por varios años.

**Trellis** a framework of light wooden or metal bars, chiefly used as a support for fruit trees or climbing plants.

Enrejado: una estructura de barras de madera o metal, usado principalmente como soporte para árboles de fruta o plantas trepadoras.

**Understory** a layer of vegetation beneath the main canopy of a forest.

Sotobosque: una capa de vegetación bajo el pabellón arbóreo de un bosque.

# A Forest of Letters
## Un bosque de letras

**Oregano**
Orégano

**Quercus**
Quercus

**Nannyberry**
*Nannyberry*

**Wood Violet**
Violetas del bosque

**Wild Rose**
Rosa silvestre

**Black Velvet Goosberry**
La grosella espinosa

**Sunflower**
Girasol

**Hazelnut**
Avellana

**Zucchini**
Calabacín

**Pear**
Pera

**Plum**
Ciruela

**Tart Cherry**
Cereza ácida

**White Wild Indigo**
Índigo blanco silvestre

**Honeyberry**
*Honeyberry*

**Redbud**
El amor de Canadá

**Daylily**
Lirio de la mañana

**Food Forest**
Bosque de alimentos

**Morel Mushroom**
Hongo morel

**Elderberry**
Baya del saúco

**Ginseng**
Ginseng

**Milkweed**
Algodoncillo

**Currant**
Grosella

**Hardy Kiwi**
Kiwi resistente

**Xąąwįsgu (Rhubarb)**
Xąąwįsgu (ruibarbo)

**Apple**
Manzana

**Juneberry**
*Juneberry*

## Apple
### Manzana

**Apples are a classic fruit.**
**Pixie Crunch is a good disease-resistant variety.**
**Choose disease resistant varieties for the best results!**

La manzana es una fruta clásica.
Pixie Crunch es una buena variedad que resiste
    a las plagas.
¡Elige variedades resistentes a las plagas
    para los mejores resultados!

# Black Velvet Gooseberry
La grosella espinosa

**These berries are easy to grow and taste great. Ouch! They do have thorns.**

Estas bayas son fáciles de sembrar y saben rico. ¡Cuidado! Tienen espinas.

# Currant
## Grosella

Currant is a fun and easy-to-grow shrub.
Black currants have an interesting flavor.
Try red, pink, and white currants too!

La grosella es un arbusto fácil y divertido de crecer.
Las grosellas negras tienen un sabor muy único.
¡Deben de probar grosellas rojas, rosadas, y
blancas también!

# Daylily
## Lirio de la mañana

**The scientific name of this flower is Hemerocallis.
All parts of the plant are edible.
Some taste better than others.**

Su nombre científico de esta flor es Hemerocallis.
Todas las partes de esta planta son comestibles.
Algunas partes saben mejor que otras.

# Elderberry
Baya del saúco

**Elderberry is a plant that is native to North America. It has edible flowers, and the fruit has medicinal qualities. The fruit is best when cooked.**

La baya del saúco es nativa de Norte América. Tiene unas flores comestibles y frutas con cualidades medicinales. La fruta sabe mejor cocida.

# Food Forest
## Bosque de alimentos

A food forest consists of a variety of plants that produce edibles in a forest setting. A food forest (or forest garden) is different from an orchard or a garden because it includes a diverse range of plants including trees and shrubs. Food forests increase food availability.

**Caution:**
Remember to eat food only from nature that you can identify.

Un bosque de alimentos consiste de una variedad de plantas que producen comestibles en un ambiente forestal. El bosque de alimentos (o jardín del bosque) es diferente de una huerta o jardín porque incluye un rango diverso de plantas incluyendo los árboles y arbustos. Estos bosques de alimento aumentan la disponibilidad de alimentos.

¡Precaución!
Recuerden que solo deben de comer alimentos de la naturaleza que se puedan identificar.

# Ginseng

Ginseng

Ginseng is a slow-growing perennial plant in the ivy family. Although the root is primarily used in traditional medicine, the berries and leaves are also safe to eat.

El ginseng es una planta perenne del género de la familia hiedra que crece lento. Aunque las raíces son usadas primeramente en la medicina tradicional, las bayas y las hojas también son comestibles.

# Hazelnut
Avellana

**Hazelnut is a yummy native plant.
Squirrels and chipmunks go nuts over this nut.**

La avellana es una planta nativa deliciosa.
Las ardillas enloquecen por estas nueces.

# White Wild Indigo
## Índigo blanco silvestre

**White Wild Indigo is a native plant that fixes nitrogen and is good for pollinators, like bees. Although bees love it, humans can't eat it.**

El índigo blanco silvestre es una planta nativa que fija nitrógeno y es buena para polinizadores como las abejas. Aunque a las abejas les encanta, los humanos no las pueden comer.

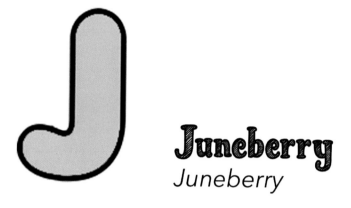

# Juneberry
*Juneberry*

**Juneberry is an easy-to-grow native fruit. They are also called Serviceberries or Shadberries. Birds, like the Cedar Waxwing, love these berries, but people can enjoy them, too.**

El *juneberry* es una fruta nativa que es fácil de sembrar. También se llaman *Serviceberries* o *Shadberries*. A los pájaros, como el *Cedar Waxwing*, les encantan estas bayas, pero los humanos también las pueden disfrutar.

# Hardy Kiwi
## Kiwi resistente

**Hardy Kiwi is a vine with small, sweet, fuzzy fruit. It needs a very sturdy trellis since the fruits are too heavy for the skinny vine.**

El kiwi resistente es una parra con una fruta chiquita, dulce, y vellosa. Requiere un enrejado robusto porque las frutas son demasiadas pesadas para la parra delgada.

# L

## Morel Mushroom
### Hongo morel

**Morel mushrooms like established forests under old apple or elm trees. You can clean them and sauté them in butter!**

*Be sure you can identify mushrooms correctly before you eat them.

A los hongos morel les gustan los bosques establecidos bajo árboles viejos de manzana u olmo. ¡Se pueden limpiar y saltear en mantequilla!

*Asegúrense de identificar que el tipo de hongo sea el correcto antes de comer.

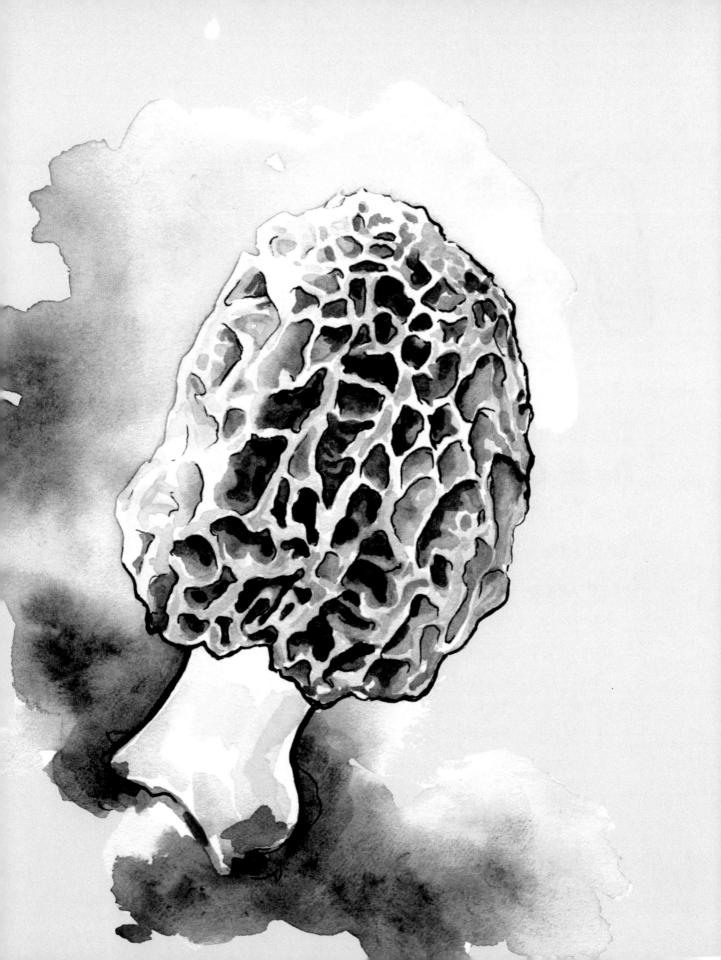

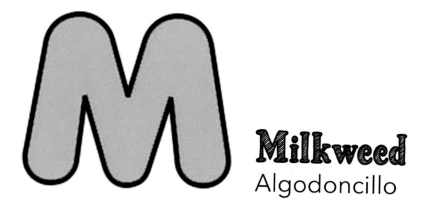

# Milkweed
## Algodoncillo

The Ho-Chunk name for milkweed is mąąhįc. The Ho-Chunk Nation has been in the Wisconsin area for thousands of years! In early summer, the Ho-Chunk collect mąąhįc flower buds and make a tasty soup.

El nombre Ho-Chunk para el algodoncillo es mąąhįc. ¡La Nación Ho-Chunk ha estado en Wisconsin por miles de años!    En el verano,  los Ho-Chunk recolectan los brotes de flores de mąąhįc y hacen una sopa deliciosa.

# Nannyberry
*Nannyberry*

**Nannyberry is a native shrub that can grow in partly shaded areas. Viburnum lentago is the scientific name. Make sure to collect some to eat before birds like the Eastern Bluebird eat them all!**

*Nannyberry* es un arbusto nativo que puede crecer en áreas de sombra parcial. El nombre científico es Viburnum lentago. Asegúrense de recolectar algunas antes de que los pájaros, como el pájaro azul oriental, se coman todas!

# Oregano
*Orégano*

Oregano makes a great groundcover, and the flowers attract pollinators. Lacewings help oregano plants by eating tiny pests called aphids.

El orégano hace una buena cobertura vegetal y las flores atraen a polinizadores. Las crisopas ayudan al orégano cuando comen plagas chiquitas que se llaman áfidos.

# Pear
Pera

Pear trees get quite tall and take up to seven years to bear fruit, but there is nothing like a perfectly ripe pear!

Árboles de peras crecen muy altos y tardan hasta siete años en dar fruto. ¡Pero no hay comparación con una pera perfectamente madura!

## Quercus
Quercus

**Quercus is the scientific name for Oak and Beech trees.**
**These trees are important plants for wildlife.**

Quercus es el nombre científico para el árbol roble y haya.
Estos árboles son importantes para la fauna silvestre.

## Redbud
El amor de Canadá

**Redbud is a native understory tree.
The flowers are edible and taste like peas.**

El amor de Canadá es un árbol nativo del sotobosque.
Las flores son comestibles y saben a chícharos.

# Sunflower
Girasol

**Sunflowers are beautiful annual flowers to plant while the trees and shrubs are young. They are great for pollinators, too.**

Los girasoles son flores anuales hermosas que se deben de plantar cuando los árboles y arbustos son jóvenes. También son muy buenas para los polinizadores.

# Tart Cherry
Cereza ácida

**North Star, Meteor, Montmorency, or Carmine Jewel are all easy varieties of cherries to grow!**

*North Star, Meteor, Montmorency, o Carmine Jewel,*
¡Todas son variedades de cerezas sencillas de sembrar!

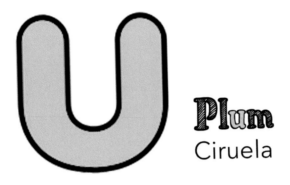

## Plum
### Ciruela

So tasty and juicy!  Wild Plum is the most
pest resistant.

¡Tan deliciosa y jugosa! Las ciruelas silvestres son
las más resistentes a las plagas.

# Wood Violet
## Violeta del bosque

**Wood Violets have edible leaves and flowers.
This useful plant also makes a great groundcover.**

Las violetas del bosque tienen hojas y flores comestibles.
Esta planta útil también hace una buena
cobertura vegetal.

# Wild Rose
## Rosa silvestre

**Wild Rose is a native flower with edible hips that attract wildlife. Humans can eat rose hips, too! It's a great source of Vitamin C.**

La rosa silvestre es una flor nativa con escaramujos comestibles que atrae a la fauna silvestre.
¡Los humanos también pueden comer escaramujos!
Es una buena fuente de vitamina C.

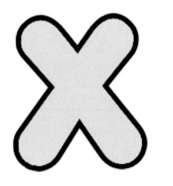

# Xąąwįsgu
## Ruibarbo

Xąąwįsgu is the Ho-Chunk word for rhubarb. Rhubarb is a vegetable even though we eat it just like a fruit. You can use the stalks to make a rhubarb pie. Just don't eat the poisonous leaves of this perennial plant.

Xąąwįsgu es la palabra Ho-Chunk para el ruibarbo. El ruibarbo es un vegetal aunque lo comemos como si fuera una fruta. Se pueden usar los tallos para hacer una tarta de ruibarbo. Simplemente no coman las hojas venenosas de esta planta perenne.

# Honeyberry
*Honeyberry*

**The honeyberry shrub blooms in March and produces tasty berries in June.
It can grow in partial shade.**

El arbusto del *honeyberry* florece en marzo y produce bayas sabrosas en junio.
Puede crecer en la sombra parcial.

## Zucchini
### Calabacín

**Zucchini is an annual that can be grown while the trees and shrubs in your newly planted food forest are young.**

El calabacín es una planta anual que puede crecer cuando los árboles y arbustos en tu bosque de alimentos son jóvenes.

 **PayPal**

Scan. Pay. Go.

# Help us plant more food forests in and around Madison, Wisconsin

#PlantTreesPlantHope

## Ayúdanos a plantar más bosques de alimentos dentro y alrededor de Madison, Wisconsin

**The true meaning of life is to plant trees, under whose shade you do not expect to sit.**

**– Nelson Henderson**

El verdadero significado de la vida es plantar árboles bajo cuya sombra no esperas sentarte.

-Nelson Henderson

# About the Authors

## Emily Schroeder

www.emilymariewatercolors.com

After teaching in elementary schools for 10 years, Emily started painting with watercolors as a way to relieve stress during the Covid pandemic. As an artist, she combines her passions for nature and man's best friend: dogs. Being bilingual and having once lived in Guadalajara, Mexico, she also translated this book into Spanish. In the future, she hopes to author and illustrate more children's books.

## Emily Steinwehe

http://emilyplants.com/

Emily is passionate about plants which led to her starting Emily Plants as well as being a co-founder of Wisconsin Food Forests. Her life's purpose is getting more plants in the ground, especially perennial, native and/or edible plants. She enjoys planting, pruning, mulching, and eating many different kinds of fruits and nuts. Her favorites include chestnuts, persimmons, hardy kiwi, gooseberries, and black raspberries.

## Erin McWalter

https://madisontrafficgarden.org/

Erin is the co-founder of Madison Traffic Garden. Her love of plants and nature has driven many plant centric projects including Wisconsin Food Forests.
"Madison Traffic Garden empowers people to participate in building their own sustainable and resilient communities. It is our passion to promote a diverse region through embracing collaboration between organizations and individuals."

## About Wisconsin Food Forests

www.wisconsinfoodforests.com

Wisconsin Food Forests is a collaboration project under Madison Traffic Garden (MTG), a nonprofit based in Madison, Wisconsin USA. Emily Steinwehe of Emily Plants and Joanna Kahvedjian of Make it Count LLC partner with MTG to plant food forests in Wisconsin. Our goal is to inspire people to engage with nature by planting more edible plants, especially trees. Building community around food sources is not only fun but very rewarding when you get to literally eat the fruits of your labor and/or labor of others. Food forests are gifts that keep on giving. We hope that people create a food forest book to teach others about what grows in their region.

Made in the USA
Monee, IL
25 May 2023

34293151R00036